FOCUS ON CURRENT EVENTS
ELECTRIC VEHICLES

by Kristina Lyn Heitkamp

FOCUS
READERS®

V☉YAGER

www.focusreaders.com

Focus Readers is distributed by North Star Editions:
sales@northstareditions.com | 888-417-0195

Produced for Focus Readers by Red Line Editorial.

Content Consultant: Dr. Eleftheria Kontou, Assistant Professor of Civil and Environmental Engineering at the University of Illinois at Urbana-Champaign

Photographs ©: Shutterstock Images, cover, 1, 8–9, 11, 13, 27, 28–29, 31, 33, 36–37, 39, 40, 45; pbpgalleries/Alamy Stock Photo, 4–5; B Christopher/Alamy Stock Photo, 7; Photo Researchers/Science History Images/Alamy Stock Photo, 14–15; Pictures Now/Alamy Stock Photo, 17; Itsuo Inouye/AP Images, 19; iStockphoto, 20–21, 23; Red Line Editorial, 25; Peter Kneffel/picture-alliance/dpa/AP Images, 35; Imaginechina/AP Images, 42–43

Library of Congress Cataloging-in-Publication Data
Names: Heitkamp, Kristina Lyn, author.
Title: Electric vehicles / by Kristina Lyn Heitkamp.
Description: Lake Elmo, MN : Focus Readers, [2022] | Series: Focus on current events | Includes index. | Audience: Grades 4-6
Identifiers: LCCN 2021040538 (print) | LCCN 2021040539 (ebook) |ISBN 9781637390771 (hardcover) | ISBN 9781637391310 (paperback) | ISBN 9781637391853 (ebook) | ISBN 9781637392324 (pdf)
Subjects: LCSH: Electric vehicles--Juvenile literature.
Classification: LCC TL220 .H45 2022 (print) | LCC TL220 (ebook) | DDC 629.22/93--dc23
LC record available at https://lccn.loc.gov/2021040538
LC ebook record available at https://lccn.loc.gov/2021040539

Printed in the United States of America
Mankato, MN
012022

ABOUT THE AUTHOR

Kristina Lyn Heitkamp is a children's book author, an environmental journalist, and a plein-air writer. She has written and edited more than 20 books and articles on many topics, including the energy industry and environmental conservation. When she's not exploring the Utah desert, she can be found plein-air writing by a river.

TABLE OF CONTENTS

CHAPTER 1

BREAKING RECORDS

In early 2019, the Genovation GXE Corvette already held the official title of the fastest street-legal electric car in the world. The GXE had reached speeds of 209 miles per hour (336 km/h). But the car was getting faster and faster with new technology. In September 2019, a driver attempted to set a new record.

The sports car took off on a 3-mile (4.8-km) runway at the Kennedy Space Center in Florida.

Genovation took a C7 Corvette Grand Sport and repurposed the car into the electric GXE Corvette.

It went from 0 to 60 miles per hour (0–97 km/h) in just seconds. After less than a minute, it was cruising above 200 miles per hour (322 km/h). The car managed to clock a top speed of 210.2 miles per hour (338.3 km/h). It had broken its own world record.

The GXE was very fast but also very quiet. That's because the car didn't have all the moving parts of a gasoline engine. Instead, five battery packs powered the electric vehicle (EV). The car's two electric motors worked silently. As a result, the vehicle gained speed without much noise or vibration.

The GXE stayed quiet even with a weight of 4,500 pounds (2,041 kg). That's more than 1,000 pounds (454 kg) heavier than a similar gasoline-powered Corvette. And the GXE could have been even heavier than that. However,

△ Genovation's first electric car came out in 2009. It was converted from an existing gasoline-powered car.

several parts of the car were made from carbon fiber, including the wheels. Carbon fiber is a lightweight material. But it is five times stronger than steel. It also provides better protection for riders. As of 2020, the automaker planned to produce only 75 GXEs. Even so, the car showed the world how far EVs had come.

CHAPTER 2

NUTS AND BOLTS

Electric vehicles come in all shapes and sizes. But there are two main kinds. All-electric vehicles (AEVs) use only electricity to run. Many AEVs use electric motors and batteries. They get power from plugging into an **electric grid**. The grid's energy can come from **renewable** sources such as wind or solar power. It can come from fossil fuels such as coal or natural gas. It can also come from nuclear energy. Regardless of where

Instead of being filled up with gasoline, electric vehicles are plugged in to charge their batteries.

the power comes from, AEVs store the electricity in batteries. AEVs run entirely on batteries, and they do not have gasoline tanks.

Plug-in **hybrid** electric vehicles (PHEVs) are the second main type. A PHEV uses both gasoline and electricity to run. It has an electric motor and a battery like an AEV. But it also has a gasoline tank and an **internal combustion** engine. A PHEV tends to use electricity first. When the battery is out of power, the car switches to the gasoline-powered engine.

Both AEVs and PHEVs use a braking system that saves energy. The system takes the **kinetic energy** from braking or from going downhill. It turns that energy into electricity. The electricity is stored in the battery for the car to use.

Many AEVs can drive 100 miles (161 km) or more on a full charge. Some models can travel much farther. Once a battery is out of power, it needs to recharge. That process can take between 30 minutes and 24 hours. This partly depends on the EV's driving range.

PARTS OF ELECTRIC VEHICLES ◄

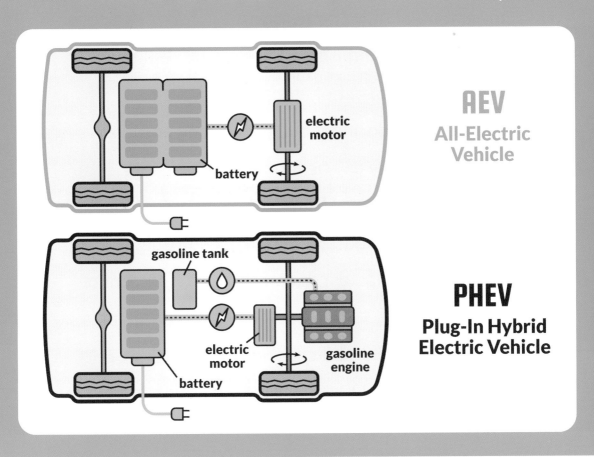

AEV
All-Electric Vehicle

electric motor

battery

gasoline tank

PHEV
Plug-In Hybrid Electric Vehicle

electric motor

gasoline engine

battery

Recharge time also depends on the type of charge. There are three types of charging. Level 1 charging is the slowest. This charging speed uses a regular outlet found in garages. Most people use a Level 1 charge at night while sleeping. That's because it can take eight hours to add enough power for just 40 miles (64 km).

Level 2 charging is faster than Level 1. It uses the same kind of outlet as clothes dryers or electric ovens do. Most public charging stations are Level 2. They can be found in parking lots or at grocery stores. Using a Level 2 charger for eight hours can add 180 miles (290 km). Level 3 charging is the fastest. It can charge 80 percent of a battery in just 30 minutes. But not all EV models can plug into a Level 3 charging station.

By the early 2020s, EVs were becoming more and more popular. Automakers were building new

▲ Fuel-cell EVs are one kind of EV. A tank (yellow) sends hydrogen to a fuel cell (silver), which produces electricity.

and improved models. And more people were buying EVs instead of gasoline-powered vehicles. However, EVs have been around for a very long time.

CHAPTER 3

HISTORY OF ELECTRIC VEHICLES

Electric vehicles existed even before gasoline-powered cars did. The ideas and inventions of many people helped make them. In 1834, a blacksmith designed an electric motor. He used the motor to move a miniature car around a track. Then, in 1859, a scientist invented the first rechargeable battery. Finally, in 1890, a chemist created the first successful EV. The vehicle used 24 batteries. It could hold six passengers, and it

An illustration shows blacksmith Thomas Davenport working on the first electric motor.

could drive up to 14 miles per hour (23 km/h). The first gasoline-powered car came along a few years later in 1893.

After that, people drove a few kinds of cars. EVs were quiet and easy to drive. Gasoline-fueled vehicles were noisy and stinky from the exhaust fumes of the engine. They were also hard to drive. Drivers had to use a hand crank to start them. In contrast, EVs started with a flip of a switch. They could travel 50 miles (80 km) on a single charge. People often used EVs for quick trips around the city. By 1900, nearly one-third of vehicles on the road were electric-powered.

However, gasoline-powered cars soon became more popular. In 1908, Ford Motor Company came out with a new gasoline-powered car. It was called the Model T. The Model T was cheaper than older gasoline-powered cars. In contrast, EVs

▲ Only wealthy people were able to afford early electric vehicles.

were expensive. Plus, most people did not have access to electricity. When oil production in Texas shot up in the 1920s, gasoline prices dropped. Gasoline became much cheaper than electricity.

In addition, Americans wanted to explore the country. They wanted cars that could drive longer distances. And they needed places to refuel on road trips. So, gasoline stations began popping up across the United States. By 1935, electric cars had nearly disappeared.

In the 1960s, scientists warned US automakers about the emissions from cars. Emissions are chemicals or substances that are released into the air. Vehicle emissions were one cause of **climate change**. The US government started limiting certain kinds of emissions in the 1970s. In 1990, those limits became stronger. They still did not limit the emissions of **greenhouse gases**. But some companies began creating electric vehicles.

In 1997, Toyota made the first mass-produced hybrid EV. It was called the Toyota Prius. In 2006,

➤ **THINK ABOUT IT**

If EVs had been more successful than gasoline-powered cars, what might transportation look like today?

A journalist takes a look at the Toyota Prius's gasoline engine (left) and its electric motor in 1997.

Tesla Motors made an electric sports car that could travel more than 200 miles (322 km) on a single charge. Interest in EVs grew along with concern about climate change. As of 2021, nearly 500 different EV models were available from more than 20 automakers.

CHAPTER 4

ADVANTAGES OF ELECTRIC VEHICLES

One advantage of electric vehicles is that they tend to be less harmful to the environment. That's because fossil-fuel-powered transportation is an enormous contributor to climate change. Gasoline-powered vehicles release greenhouse gases into the air. These gases become trapped in Earth's atmosphere. This raises Earth's average temperature. The rising temperature is causing a climate crisis around the world. Its effects include

In 2020, transportation was a top contributor of greenhouse gas emissions in the United States. It produced 29 percent of US emissions.

heat waves, flooding, and drought. In addition, the exhaust from gasoline-powered vehicles is dangerous for humans. Air pollution from cars increases the likelihood of asthma and heart problems.

Scientists often judge a vehicle's climate impact based on its emissions. And there are two types of vehicle emissions. These types are direct emissions and life-cycle emissions. Direct emissions are the pollution that comes out of a vehicle while it's driving. Life-cycle emissions include all the emissions that come from making and using the car. For example, gasoline needs to be drilled, pumped, and transported. These steps

> ➤ THINK ABOUT IT

How is climate change affecting the area where you live?

Direct vehicle emissions are often called tailpipe emissions.

all create emissions. Cars also require many kinds of materials. Machines turn those materials into car parts. Those processes create emissions, too.

Gasoline-powered vehicles create both direct emissions and life-cycle emissions. In contrast, EVs produce zero direct emissions. However, they do produce life-cycle emissions. That's because producing electricity creates emissions. In 2020, 60 percent of electricity in the United

States came from fossil fuels. Only 20 percent of electricity was renewable. Even so, the emissions from making electricity were still much lower than emissions from using gasoline. In 2021, scientists calculated that US emissions would drop significantly if all Americans switched to EVs.

Overall, driving EVs tends to cost less than driving gasoline-powered cars. For one thing, recharging an EV is cheaper than filling up a gasoline tank. The cost of electricity often gets cheaper at night, when fewer people are using it. Plus, the average rates for electricity usually do not change much. In contrast, gasoline and oil prices tend to change often. In addition, there are fewer moving parts inside an EV. This makes an EV easier and cheaper to maintain.

Some people report other advantages as well. Driving an EV can feel different from driving a gasoline-powered vehicle. For example, AEVs provide instant power. They move faster in a shorter time than gasoline-powered cars. EVs also offer a smooth and quiet drive. The batteries are stored on the floor of the car. This helps the car hug the road for a comfortable drive. Some people say they prefer these driving experiences.

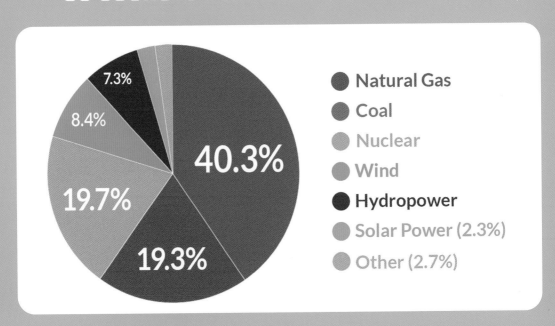

US SOURCES FOR ELECTRICITY IN 2020

- 40.3%
- 19.3%
- 19.7%
- 8.4%
- 7.3%

- Natural Gas
- Coal
- Nuclear
- Wind
- Hydropower
- Solar Power (2.3%)
- Other (2.7%)

ELECTRIC VEHICLES FOR EVERYONE

In the United States, climate change affects some communities more than others. The crisis has been most harmful to low-income communities and communities of color. Extreme weather events tend to affect these communities more. That's partly because it can be too expensive to repair damage. These communities are also more likely to live near freeways and factories. As a result, they are more often exposed to pollution.

For these reasons, many US lawmakers are working to help. In California, the Clean Cars 4 All program helps low-income people swap out old gasoline-powered cars. In return, they get electric vehicles. Californians in places with poor air quality can receive money to buy an EV. Or they can get money to use public transportation.

▲ Black people are approximately 40 percent more likely than white people to experience asthma.

At the national level, a lawmaker put forth a bill in early 2020. The bill was aimed at the US Department of Energy. It would have the department build 200,000 EV charging stations in **underserved** communities by 2030. The stations would be near public parking spaces, apartments, and public housing. Building these stations would provide more charging access. Building them would also provide many jobs.

CHAPTER 5

ROOM FOR IMPROVEMENT

Experts predict that electric vehicles could rule the roads by the 2050s. However, this change will bring new challenges. For example, one study found that the need for electricity could increase 38 percent between 2020 and 2050. The study found that EVs will likely be a big part of the increase. As a result, electric grids will need to be improved. They must be designed to handle the rising electricity demand.

Electric grids are massive networks that use power lines to bring electricity from power plants into homes.

Electricity needs change throughout the day. People use the most electricity in the early evening. If too many people charge their EVs during this time, electric grids could get overloaded. Then many people would lose power.

Some states are already facing strains on their grids. In 2020, California experienced an extreme heat wave. To keep cool, many people turned on air conditioners. Electric grids weren't able to handle the rise in demand. So, electric companies used rolling blackouts. That's when different areas lose power over a stretch of time. In February 2021, many Texans faced a total blackout. That's when everyone in a large area loses power. The state's temperatures hit record lows. The cold caused a sudden rise in demand for heat. Many power sources also froze, especially natural gas. So, the electric grids had much less supply.

As EVs become more common, blackouts could have greater impacts.

As climate change worsens, extreme weather events will increase. They will put more stress on electric **infrastructure**. This could have several effects on EVs. First, extreme temperatures can affect EV batteries. For instance, cold temperatures can reduce battery life. Second, EVs would not be able to charge during blackouts. If people need to evacuate during an emergency, EVs might not have enough stored energy.

In fact, charging is one of the main problems facing EVs. People need charging stations to be nearby. But in 2020, the number of public electric charging stations was low. For EVs to succeed, people need to build many more public charging stations. Charging time is another challenge. Recharging an EV can take hours. Most public charging stations are located at workplaces, parking lots, or grocery stores. Recharging at a workplace for eight hours could be an option for many people. But recharging at a store for eight hours might not make sense.

In 2020, more than 80 percent of EV charging happened at home. People often charge their cars overnight in garages. However, many people live in homes without garages. For example, they might live in an apartment building. Or they may have to park on the street. Without nearby public

▲ Certain electrical wiring can help homes better handle charging EVs.

stations, people could struggle to keep their cars charged.

Experts believe that these problems can be addressed. But they will require careful planning. For example, planners need to figure out the best locations for new charging stations. And stations near highways will need high-speed chargers.

THE FUTURE OF GASOLINE STATIONS

In 2021, there were more than 136,000 gasoline stations in the United States. These shops sell snacks, drinks, and gasoline for vehicles. But as electric vehicles became more popular, some gasoline stations were no longer needed. Retired stations have become auto shops, hair salons, and coffee shops. Some people believe that old gasoline stations should be made into neighborhood gathering spots. But one gasoline station owner decided to switch to an electric charging station.

In 2019, a gasoline station in Takoma Park, Maryland, made the change. It was the first fully converted gasoline-to-electric charging station in the United States. It wasn't cheap to pull up the gasoline storage tanks. But the owner got grant

△ Transitioning to EVs requires lots of work. So, the process can provide many people with clean and well-paying jobs.

money to help pay for it. The city needed more electric charging stations. There were only two other stations in the area.

The new fueling station has four chargers. Drivers can wait inside the convenience store. The store uses automatic machines to deliver snacks and drinks. The shop also has screens where drivers can watch their vehicles' charging progress.

CHAPTER 6

GREEN CHALLENGES

Many climate experts stress the importance of moving toward a green economy. A green economy would use fewer fossil fuels. It would also make eco-friendly and humane choices when developing new technologies. Electric vehicles will be part of any green economy. But there are still environmental and social costs in making and using EVs. For example, more work is needed to limit EVs' life-cycle emissions. EVs require fossil

The production of EVs in factories is one part of their life-cycle emissions.

fuels in their design and distribution. Coal is used to melt the steel for the bodies of the cars. Diesel oil is used to ship parts across oceans.

Most EV batteries are made with a metal called lithium. Wind turbines and solar panels also use this metal. Most of Earth's lithium is found in Bolivia, Argentina, and Chile. Drilling for lithium uses large amounts of water. Water is limited in these dry regions. Farmers and ranchers compete with lithium mining for water. As a result, they can't always get the water they need.

Cobalt is another metal used in EV batteries, wind turbines, and solar panels. Nearly half of the world's cobalt supply is found in the Democratic Republic of the Congo. Human rights organizations report that cobalt mining in the country can be deadly. Mining also often uses child labor. In addition, toxic minerals can

▲ Earth's largest single source of lithium is under the Salar de Uyuni in Bolivia. This salt flat can be seen from space.

leak into rivers and streams. The environmental damage from cobalt mining lasts hundreds of years. This pollution affects local communities the most.

Most of these materials are found in developing nations. As demand for materials increases, mining will likely affect global relations. Wealthy nations have often exploited the resources and workers of developing nations. For example,

⚠ Lithium battery packs are made up of many individual battery cells.

mining often takes place in developing nations. But most of the profit goes to wealthy countries. However, this process could change. Developing nations could use their own resources for their own growth. And people in wealthy nations could demand their governments stop unfair practices.

EVs also have their own problems of waste. For example, a lithium battery typically lasts for 8 to

12 years in an EV. After that, the battery can no longer power the vehicle. As EVs gain popularity, millions of EV batteries will become spent. Like all batteries, they can be harmful if they are thrown away. Their toxic metals can pollute the environment. Lithium batteries can also explode or catch fire.

However, EV batteries can be recycled. Even better, used EV batteries can still store electricity. So, they could provide energy storage for other things. Repurposing a battery can be costly and take a lot of time. But it is more eco-friendly than simply throwing the battery away.

THINK ABOUT IT ◁

In addition to using EVs instead of gasoline-powered vehicles, how else can people reduce greenhouse gas emissions?

CHAPTER 7

BEYOND CARS

Passenger cars receive much of the attention when it comes to electric vehicles. But other vehicles play huge roles in society. For example, buses provide affordable transportation for millions of people. And **paratransit** vehicles often make travel easier for people with disabilities.

As of 2021, however, most of these vehicles were still gasoline-powered. China was home to nearly all the world's electric buses. Even so,

The entire bus system of Shenzhen, China, is electric. It includes more than 16,000 electric buses.

China still depended mostly on gasoline-powered buses. Many cities are working to use more electric buses. But experts argue that cities often need national support. Cities also need transit and energy providers to work together.

Climate experts say that semitrucks should also be electrified. These vehicles deliver all kinds of goods. A single semitruck can travel more than 65,000 miles (104,607 km) per year. As a result, semitrucks produce approximately 7 percent of global greenhouse gas emissions.

Automakers are developing electric trucks. However, few were on the road as of 2021. That's partly because semitrucks carry heavy loads for long distances. As a result, the trucks need large, heavy batteries. Those batteries are often expensive. But during the 2010s, the cost of large batteries dropped. In fact, in 2021, some

Tesla's Semi is designed to quickly reach highway speeds while carrying an 80,000-pound (36,000-kg) load.

scientists argued that electric trucks were already the cheapest long-term option.

Other kinds of EVs were making progress, too. For example, an all-electric plane flew for 30 minutes in 2020. The pilot was the only person onboard. Most scientists believed electric passenger planes were still decades away. Nevertheless, EVs had come a long way. And new developments were just around the corner.

ELECTRIC VEHICLES

Write your answers on a separate piece of paper.

1. Write a letter to your local government about the benefits of using electric vehicles.

2. If you could buy a new car, would you buy an electric vehicle or a gasoline-powered car? Why?

3. When was the first successful electric vehicle built?

    A. 1890

    B. 1935

    C. 1997

4. Why do all-electric vehicles still produce greenhouse gas emissions?

    A. All-electric vehicles use gasoline when their batteries are low on charge.

    B. The electricity that powers all-electric vehicles always comes from fossil fuels.

    C. The process of building an all-electric vehicle relies on fossil fuels.

Answer key on page 48.

GLOSSARY

climate change
A human-caused global crisis involving long-term changes in Earth's temperature and weather patterns.

electric grid
A complex network that delivers electricity from power sources to users.

greenhouse gases
Gases that trap heat in Earth's atmosphere, causing climate change.

hybrid
Having multiple systems that do similar jobs.

infrastructure
The structures, such as roads and bridges, that a city needs to function.

internal combustion
Burning air and fuel inside an engine to generate power.

kinetic energy
Energy that an object has because of its motion.

paratransit
Services that add to public transit systems by providing rides for individuals, often not on a regular schedule.

renewable
Having to do with natural resources that never run out.

underserved
Not having access to the same services and resources as other areas.

TO LEARN MORE

BOOKS

Allen, John. *Thinking Critically: Electric Cars*. San Diego: ReferencePoint Press, 2019.

Fallon, Michael. *Self-Driving Cars: The New Way Forward*. Minneapolis: Lerner Publishing, 2019.

Klepeis, Alicia. *The Future of Transportation: From Electric Cars to Jet Packs*. North Mankato, MN: Capstone Press, 2020.

NOTE TO EDUCATORS

Visit **www.focusreaders.com** to find lesson plans, activities, links, and other resources related to this title.

INDEX

Answer Key: 1. Answers will vary; **2.** Answers will vary; **3.** A; **4.** C